Pablo Pica...

Pablo Picasso's Noël

Carol Ann Duffy

Illustrated by Léa Maupetit

PICADOR

First published 2017 by Picador
an imprint of Pan Macmillan
20 New Wharf Road, London N1 9RR
Associated companies throughout the world
www.panmacmillan.com

ISBN 978-1-5098-4819-5

Manufactured in Italy

Visit *www.picador.com* to read more about all our books
and to buy them. You will also find features, author interviews and
news of any author events, and you can sign up for e-newsletters
so that you're always first to hear about our new releases.

For Imtiaz
Remembering Simon

A sweet winter light blushed
as Pablo Picasso walked with his dog
under the cypress trees
and the bell of the old chapel guessed at the hour.
It was Christmas Eve.

The scent of rosemary
gifted the cold air and he felt his heart
lift with a *joie de vivre*
that had made his art the world's exuberant twin –
everything to win.

The dog cartooned for home,
Le Mas Notre-Dame-de-Vie; the chauffeur
smoked by the Oldsmobile,
the lamps of Mougins whispering on below
and a daub of moon.

Then the Maestro was there,
grinning, rubbing his hands, as the dog barked
and they jumped in the back;
only a goat munching the grass seeing them leave
in the pastel dusk.

Down the labyrinth lanes
went the Minotaur, as the olive groves
engraved their silvered ghosts.
His eyes were the eyes of God, the eyes of an owl,
widening for Mougins.

So Picasso and dog
entered the bar at the top of town,
while the chauffeur brought in
a bag of crayons, brushes and paints from the car
and the drinkers clapped.

Firstly, he drew his glass
on the tablecloth, then crayoned the wine,
the glow of its beige pink;
the bottle, its *Torch of Medusa* lines and curves
beautifully female.

Even lovelier though,
the barmaid resting her chin on her arms,
accepting his strong gaze
as he sketched her face, tousling her ebony hair
with a smudge of thumb.

The proprietor came
with olives and canapés. He drew them.
A thin musician played
a carol. He drew him; wooing his plump guitar,
smitten with music.

Allez! He stood to go,
So did they all – le boucher, boulanger,
le fabricant de chandelier
dispersing red candles from each of his pockets
to burn and follow.

The hills giggled in light
across the valley; the mountains scumbled
with snow; and Picasso
led the fervent procession up to the Town Square;
the Christmas Tree there.

Outside at the cafe,
he painted plates – anointed them owls,
bulls, boys, girls, Spanish suns.
And the town choir sang by the mirthful tree, praising
his pure alchemy.

Give us a warm fire, Lord.
Alegre, Alegre, God give us joy.
Noël – all will be blessed.
And if this coming year there are no more of us,
may there be no less.

Then to *Le Feu Follet*
for a feast, where, sipping aperitifs
facing the small Town Hall,
Picasso leapt up to paint the dove of peace
on its honeyed wall.

Shooting stars! He toasted
Cézanne, Van Gogh, Apollinaire – *mes frères* –
while from the restaurant
the accordion player squeezed *La Vie en Rose*
then Picasso chose:

a lobster, which frightened
the curious restaurant cat; blue claws
snapping the air, mad clack
on the plate as Picasso slashed with his crayons
and captured it whole;

then twelve oysters on ice,
which reminded him of his friend Matisse;
how he painted the smell
painted the taste of the ocean's flesh in the mouth.
And this made him smile.

A boy in a white shirt,
shy, came to Picasso's table and bowed
and Monsieur Picasso
painted an octopus on his shirt, both long sleeves
dangling in water.

More! He folded and tore
then unfolded the paper tablecloth –
voilà! – held it aloft,
transformed into friezes of dancers and dogs
and all took a scrap.

He drew the maître d',
the sommelier and his wife, the chef,
the waiters, the diners
and, old man in the mirror there, washing his hands,
his last self-portrait.

He sketched from the church steps
as the townsfolk carolled to midnight mass
and he drew against death,
the ending of light; watching a boy lead a lamb
to the Christmas hour.

Then he left his great gifts,
climbed in the dark waiting car with his dog,
eyes priming the blank moon.
Mes enfants, remember the Noël Picasso
drew, painted the town.

Also by Carol Ann Duffy and available from Picador

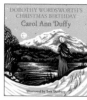